More Object Lessons
for Very Young Children

Object Lessons Series

Bess, C. W., *Children's Object Sermons for the Seasons,* 1026-8

Bess, C. W., *Object-Centered Children's Sermons,* 0734-8

Bess, C. W., *Sparkling Object Sermons for Children,* 0824-7

Bess, C. W., & Roy DeBrand, *Bible-Centered Object Sermons for Children,* 0886-7

Biller, Tom & Martie, *Simple Object Lessons for Children,* 0793-3

Bruinsma, Sheryl, *Easy-to-Use Object Lessons,* 0832-8

Bruinsma, Sheryl, *New Object Lessons,* 0775-5

Bruinsma, Sheryl, *Object Lessons for Every Occasion,* 0994-4

Bruinsma, Sheryl, *Object Lessons for Special Days,* 0920-0

Bruinsma, Sheryl, *Object Lessons for Very Young Children,* 0956-1

Claassen, David, *Object Lessons for a Year,* 2514-1

Connelly, H. W., *47 Object Lessons for Youth Programs,* 2314-9

Coombs, Robert, *Concise Object Sermons for Children,* 2541-9

Coombs, Robert, *Enlightening Object Lessons for Children,* 2567-2

Cooper, Charlotte, *50 Object Stories for Children,* 2523-0

Cross, Luther, *Easy Object Stories,* 2502-8

Cross, Luther, *Object Lessons for Children,* 2315-7

Cross, Luther, *Story Sermons for Children,* 2328-9

De Jonge, Joanne, *More Object Lessons from Nature,* 3004-8

De Jonge, Joanne, *Object Lessons from Nature,* 2989-9

De Jonge, Joanne, *Object Lessons from Your Home and Yard,* 3026-9

Edstrom, Lois, *Contemporary Object Lessons for Children's Church,* 3432-9

Gebhardt, Richard, & Mark Armstrong, *Object Lessons from Science Experiments,* 3811-1

Godsey, Kyle, *Object Lessons About God,* 3841-3

Hendricks, William, *Object Lessons Based on Bible Characters,* 4373-5

Hendricks, William, & Merle Den Bleyker, *Object Lessons from Sports and Games,* 4134-1

Hendricks, William, & Merle Den Bleyker, *Object Lessons That Teach Bible Truths,* 4172-4

Loeks, Mary, *Object Lessons for Children's Worship,* 5584-9

McDonald, Roderick, *Successful Object Sermons,* 6270-5

Runk, Wesley, *Object Lessons from the Bible,* 7698-6

Squyres, Greg, *Simple Object Lessons for Young Children,* 8330-3

Sullivan, Jessie, *Object Lessons and Stories for Children's Church,* 8037-1

Sullivan, Jessie, *Object Lessons with Easy-to-Find Objects,* 8190-4

Trull, Joe, *40 Object Sermons for Children,* 8831-3

More Object Lessons
for Very Young Children

by Sheryl Bruinsma

Baker Books

A Division of Baker Book House Co
Grand Rapids, Michigan 49516

©1994 by Sheryl Bruinsma

Published by Baker Books
a division of Baker Book House Company
P.O. Box 6287, Grand Rapids, MI 49516-6287

ISBN 0-8010-1075-6

Printed in the United States of America

Unless otherwise indicated, Scripture quotations are from the New King
James Version. Copyright © 1979, 1980, 1982, Thomas Nelson, Inc.,
Publishers.

With love to my grandchildren
Daniel, Christina, Megan, and Sean

Contents

Using Object Lessons to Teach the Three-to-Five-Year-Old Child

Like the parables in the Bible, object lessons remain a very effective way to present spiritual truths. This is especially true for children because they learn abstract concepts more easily if presented with a concrete example. Objects also accomplish a more important feat—they get the child's attention.

Very young children present a special challenge. There are several things to keep in mind while teaching the three-to-five-year-olds. Keep the object simple so the children can understand the comparison. Speak in their vocabulary so that they will understand what you are saying. Keep the lesson brief to fit their short attention span. Use the object to keep their attention. Use your voice to emphasize concepts and hold their interest.

A more complete section on teaching very young children can be found in my fourth book of object lessons titled *Object Lessons for Very Young Children,* published by Baker Book House in 1988.

Remember, never underestimate the ability of a very young child to begin to understand spiritual concepts. Sometimes children's uncluttered minds grasp eagerly the truths that elude adults. Would that we all could approach spiritual realities with childlike openness and faith.

The Beatitudes

Jesus gave us eight wonderful keys to happiness. We can share these with children and orient their unfolding lives in these directions.

Even though they can be presented separately, the Beatitudes in this section are given as a series with reference made to the preceding lessons. It is suggested that eight large paper keys be cut out and a lesson printed on each key. This will help reinforce the lessons. The words printed on the keys will serve as reminders for the person presenting the lesson, while a sketch or drawing of the object used for each lesson will remind the children. The eight lessons are the following:

1. Happy are those who need God.
2. Happy are those who can cry and feel better.
3. Happy are those who are helpful.
4. Happy are those who want what is good.
5. Happy are those who are kind to others.
6. Happy are those who keep their hearts clean.
7. Happy are those who make peace.
8. Happy are those who do what is right.

It is a good idea to review the concept of the Beatitudes as keys to happiness at the beginning of each lesson. Reference to the numbers of the Beatitudes on the keys provides continuity.

Remember to keep everything simple and to speak in the children's language.

The First Beatitude

Scripture: Blessed are the poor in spirit, for theirs is the kingdom of heaven (Matt. 5:3).

Object: Two clear cups or glasses; colored liquid such as chocolate milk or fruit juice (fill one glass about one-half and the other about three-fourths)

Lesson: If you think your cup is already full, you will not receive more of what God has for you.

Outline

Begin by introducing the concept of the Beatitudes and the first key: "Happy are those who need God."

Introduce object: These two glasses of chocolate milk will help me tell you about the first key to happiness. Listen.
1. Fuller glass: "I'm best. I have the most."
2. Other glass: "I've shared, so I need to go back to God for more."
3. Which glass would God choose? The one that needs more from him.

Conclusion: You will have real happiness if you know that you need to keep going back to God to have more of all the wonderful things he has for you.

In the next several lessons I am going to be talking to you about a part in the Bible called the Beatitudes. The Beatitudes are eight keys to happiness. They each start with the words *Blessed are*. *Blessed are* means "Happy are." We use the word *happy* a lot. The "blessed are" kind of happiness is better than the regular happiness, which comes and goes. Sometimes you are happy about something, and when it is over you forget about it. The "blessed are" kind of happiness is deep down inside of you and doesn't go away. Now let's look at the first key to the "blessed are" kind of happiness: "Happy are those who need God."

These two glasses of chocolate milk will help me tell you about the first key to happiness. Listen.

"Hi there, boys and girls. [*Move the glass slightly from side to side as if it were moving and talking.*] Look at how full I am. I have much more in me than that glass over there. I'm so great. I don't need anybody or anything. Pity that other glass that doesn't have as much as I do, because I am better! God must love me the most."

"Hi, I'm a glass, too. I do not have as much in me as that glass over there because a little boy just had a drink from me. I need to go back to God for more. Every time I go to God, he has more to give me. I don't ever have to worry about how full I am, because God keeps giving me more and more. I'll let someone else have a drink and then I'll go back to God for some more."

Now, boys and girls, which glass do you think is best? Which glass do you think God likes the best? Yes, the one that knows it needs to come back to God for more.

The Beatitude says, "Blessed are the poor in spirit, for theirs is the kingdom of heaven." It is talking about our spirit, the part inside of us that loves God. We should be willing to share that love so we can go back to God for more. Our spirits need God. If our spirits really want what God has to give, we won't say, "I have enough. Look at how great I am."

You will have real happiness if you know that you need to keep going back to God for more of the wonderful things he has for you.

The Second Beatitude

Scripture: Blessed are those who mourn, for they shall be comforted (Matt. 5:4).

Object: disinfectant and bandages

Lesson: It's all right to cry. God made us that way.

Outline

Introduce the second key: "Happy are those who can cry and feel better."

Introduce object: When you get hurt and start to bleed, what does someone do to help you? Yes, the person gets something to wash it off and then puts a bandage on it.

1. Wash off the sore with disinfectant. Wash off the hurt that is on the inside with tears.
2. Put a bandage on the sore. A hug is a bandage for the hurt on the inside.
3. You can't see a hurt on the inside, but it is just as important to take care of it as to take care of a hurt on the outside.

Conclusion: You will have real happiness, because the inside hurt won't get worse, it will get better.

Today we are going to talk some more about the "blessed are" keys to happiness. The second key is the one we are going to talk about today. It says: "Happy are those who can cry and feel better."

When you get hurt and start to bleed, what does someone do to help you? Yes, the person gets something to wash it off and then puts a bandage on it. You need to wash off a sore so that it will not get infected. The germs need to be washed off or more germs will grow and make the sore worse. Something like this happens when you get hurt inside as well. You need to "wash off" the hurt before it becomes infected or gets worse. You can't swallow this disinfectant to wash off a sore on the inside, but you can cry. Your tears will help to wash it. This key to happiness says that it is okay to cry because it makes you feel better.

After your sore is clean, it needs a bandage. When you have a hurt on the inside, it needs a bandage as well. Hugs are bandages. They make the hurt feel better.

People know if you have fallen down and hurt yourself. They can see the sore. They can see it bleed. They will help you. People can't always see the hurt on the inside. You need to tell them that it is there. You need to cry and talk about what is hurting you. That way they can help you. They can give you a hug and help you with your problem. If you don't cry and you don't say anything and nobody knows you are hurting, the hurt will get worse. It will keep you from being happy. That is why the second Beatitude says: "Blessed are those who mourn, for they shall be comforted." To mourn is to cry and let people know what is bothering you. That way you can get the comfort or help and hugs that you need for the "blessed are" kind of happiness.

You will have real happiness because the hurt won't get worse, it will get better.

3

The Third Beatitude

Scripture: Blessed are the meek, for they shall inherit the earth (Matt. 5:5).

Object: A large cutout of each blade of a scissors with a hole punched to insert a small nut and bolt, or a scissors which can be taken apart (in a hurry, an intact scissors can be used by holding one blade at a time upright); piece of paper

Lesson: God loves the humble, stable, kind Christian.

Outline

Introduce the third key: "Happy are those who are helpful."
Introduce object: I have a really big pair of scissors here.
  1. Both scissor blades talk about how important they are.
  2. The little nut and bolt holds them together so they can work.
  3. Meek people are those who do the little things and don't expect others to know.
Conclusion: The meek have deep-down happiness because they don't do things just so that others will tell them how wonderful they are.

T oday we are going to talk about the third key to happiness that Jesus gave us in the Bible: "Happy are those who are helpful."

I have a really big pair of scissors here. The blades come apart when I take out this little nut and bolt.

"Look at me! Look at me! [*Talk in a sing-song voice while strutting the scissor blade.*] I'm sharp as a knife and I can cut anything. Oh, everybody can see what a good job I can do."

The second scissor blade says, "I'm just as big and just as sharp and just as important as you are. Give me a piece of paper and I'll show you how good I am. Watch me cut this paper. Hm-m, I seem to be having a little trouble here."

"What's your problem?" the first scissor blade says. "I can do a better job than that. Let me try."

While the two scissor blades are trying to cut the paper, the little nut and bolt arrives. "Excuse me, please. Perhaps I could help you both. If you would let me take my place in those little holes, I could hold you together while you get the job done." [*Assemble scissors and make cutting motions or cut paper.*]

Each of the scissor blades was bragging, but neither one of them could have done the job without the little nut and bolt holding them together. Did you hear the little nut and bolt bragging? No, it was just happy that the scissors was able to work again. It was meek, steady, and reliable without needing people to tell it how wonderful it was.

The third Beatitude says: "Blessed are the meek, for they shall inherit the earth." It means that real happiness is for the people who want to do little things without bragging. They don't need people to tell them how great they are. God will reward them. He will give them the best thing there is on the whole earth—true, inside, lasting happiness.

They will have deep-down happiness because they don't do things just so that others will tell them how wonderful they are.

The Fourth Beatitude

Scripture: Blessed are those who hunger and thirst for righteousness, for they shall be filled (Matt. 5:6).

Object: an empty plate

Lesson: Search for truth and goodness and you will find it as well as happiness.

Outline

Introduce the fourth key: "Happy are those who want what is good."

Introduce object: If you were really hungry, what would you like to see on this plate?

1. A healthy body needs good food to eat.
2. A healthy mind and spirit need good things as well.
3. Fill your spirit with truth, kindness, gentleness, and love.

Conclusion: When you want good things you will fill your spirit with good thoughts and feelings, and you will feel full with real happiness.

These are the keys to happiness. Keys are used to unlock treasures. Happiness is the best treasure we can have. The fourth key says: "Happy are those who want what is good."

If you were really hungry, what would you like to see on this plate? Pizza, spaghetti, peanut butter and jelly sandwiches? Those foods along with fruits and vegetables would keep your stomach and your body quite happy. I'm glad that is what you want.

What about your spirit, the part of you that loves and feels? For what would it be hungry? What would you want your mind, the part of you that thinks, to have? It can't eat the regular food like your body needs. You can't put its food on this plate, but we can talk about it. Do you think you would have a healthy spirit if it wanted things like kicking and hitting and saying mean things and listening to bad stories? No, it would get sick on that. Is it good for your mind to think about being angry and getting even with someone? No, that's not good "food" for it either.

Let's think of good things, like sharing. How about being kind and helpful? What about a smile and a gentle word? How about loving and hugging? Wanting good things for your spirit also comes from Bible stories, thinking about God, and praying to God. Doesn't just talking about these things make you feel better? It makes me feel better.

That's what the fourth Beatitude means: "Blessed are those who hunger and thirst for righteousness, for they shall be filled." Righteousness is wanting to do good things like telling the truth, being kind, and showing love. When you want to do good things you will fill your spirit with good thoughts and feelings, and you will feel full with real happiness.

5

The Fifth Beatitude

Scripture: Blessed are the merciful, for they shall obtain mercy (Matt. 5:7).

Object: a bowl of candy (or anything that a child might be tempted not to share)

Lesson: Those who give kindness and compassion will receive happiness.

Outline

Introduce the fifth key: "Happy are those who are kind to others."

Introduce object: I have a bowl filled with candy for one lucky person.

1. Give the bowl to one child.
2. People who share are happier.
3. Sharing, thinking of others first, brings happiness.

Conclusion: That way everybody is happy, but the person who showed kindness first is the happiest.

This is our fifth key to happiness: "Happy are those who are kind to others." I have a bowl filled with candy for one lucky person. Let's see, who shall it be? How about Danny! Here, Danny, you may have this bowl of candy all to yourself. The rest of you say that isn't fair? Well, life isn't fair, but let's see what Danny does with the candy. Are you going to eat all of it by yourself in front of your friends? [*Have enough candy so Danny can share with the others.*]

I'm glad you want to share the candy, Danny. I don't think you would have enjoyed it with all these sad faces looking at you.

Doesn't sharing and making people happy give you a warm feeling inside? Kindness is catching too. When you are kind to others, it makes them want to be kind themselves.

The fifth Beatitude says: "Blessed are the merciful, for they shall obtain mercy." Mercy means being kind even when you don't have to be. It makes other people happy, and that gives you a warm, happy feeling. It also pleases God to see you being kind and thoughtful.

That way everybody is happy, but the person who showed kindness first is the happiest.

6

The Sixth Beatitude

Scripture: Blessed are the pure in heart, for they shall see God (Matt. 5:8).

Object: a glass of clean water and a glass of very dirty water (glass can contain ingredients such as vinegar, leftover food, dirt, coffee, etc.)

Lesson: Keep your heart and mind pure.

Outline

Introduce the sixth key: "Happy are those who keep their hearts clean."

Introduce object: Look at these two glasses. Who will come here and take a drink from each of them?

1. You need good, clean water to drink. Your heart needs good clean things also.
2. The glass of bad stuff can make you sick. Bad stuff can make your heart sick and unhappy.

Conclusion: A sick heart is a sad heart, but you will have real happiness if you keep your heart clean and healthy.

Today we are going to talk about keeping our hearts pure or clean. The sixth key says: "Happy are those who keep their hearts clean."

Look at these two glasses. Who will come here and take a drink from each of them? Raise your hand if you would be willing to take a drink from this glass of pure, clean water. Now raise your hand if you would like to take a drink from this other glass. It does look bad, doesn't it? There's no telling what is in this glass. I'm glad you're smart enough not to want to drink this stuff. It could make you sick.

You shouldn't drink this glass of bad-looking stuff. It could poison you. Your heart, inside of you where you love, can get poisoned, too. You can put bad stuff in your heart, and it will get sick and not work right. You can't be happy with a sick heart. Your mind told you not to drink from this glass. Your mind can also tell you what not to let go into your heart. To keep your heart clean and healthy, it needs clean, kind, gentle, good, loving, happy, thankful, forgiving things—like the pure, clean water in this glass. If you put bad things like hating, fighting, swearing, being proud, or being greedy into your heart, it will get sick.

This is very important to remember as you are growing up, because there are plenty of bad things in the world that would like to get into your heart. You need to say, "No, I don't want that going into me. I'm going to let only good things into my heart." This Beatitude says: "Blessed are the pure in heart, for they shall see God." Keep your heart pure like this glass of clean water that you can see right through. See my hand? If your heart is pure, you can see, or know and understand God, and be happy.

A sick heart is a sad heart, but you will have real happiness if you keep your heart clean and healthy.

7

The Seventh Beatitude

Scripture: Blessed are the peacemakers, for they shall be called [the children] of God (Matt. 5:9).

Object: an object to tear or break; tape or glue to fix it

Lesson: God wants his children to be peacemakers.

Outline

Introduce the seventh key: "Happy are those who make peace." (Define peace.)

Introduce object: I brought some tape to help me explain what I mean.

1. When something breaks we can fix it before people get angry.
2. When people are upset, we can talk to them and try to keep them from being mean to each other.

Conclusion: God will be pleased to say, "There is one of my children doing good work by making peace."

The seventh key to happiness says: "Happy are those who make peace." Does anyone know what peace is? Sometimes when it is very noisy, somebody might yell, "I need a little peace and quiet." In that case making peace means to quiet down and not bother other people. You can all do that, can't you? Making peace also means fixing things that are bothering people so that they won't get upset and start fighting.

24

I brought some tape to help me explain what I mean. This picture is a favorite of mine. I would feel bad if anything happened to it. What if I let you look at it and it got torn accidentally? That would make me very upset [*make small tear*]. Now, if you were a peacemaker, you would want to do something to keep things from getting out of hand. What might you do to this paper to make me feel better? Yes, you could put a piece of tape on the back and fix it so that the tear doesn't even show. You would probably say something to me like, "It's all right now. Look, you can't even see the tear. Don't be upset." Peacemakers do what they can to fix what happened; they try to make people feel better.

Why do peacemakers do this? They know that God doesn't like people fighting—especially over things like this that are not even important.

Now, what if John took my paper and tore it on purpose? That's where things get hard for the person making peace. I would keep feeling upset about my picture until John said he was sorry. What could the peacemaker do? Yes, he could ask John why he tore my picture. That would make John stop to think about what he did. I think that's better than just telling John to say he is sorry.

By the time we got the problem all settled, you would be a pretty tired peacemaker. It's not easy work, but today's Beatitude says: "Blessed are the peacemakers, for they shall be called [the children] of God." God will be pleased to say, "There is one of my children doing good work by making peace."

The Eighth Beatitude

Scripture: Blessed are those who are persecuted for righteousness' sake, for theirs is the kingdom of heaven (Matt. 5:10).

Object: a "Book of Life"

Lesson: Those who are persecuted for righteousness will receive their reward in heaven.

Outline

Introduce the final key: "Happy are those who do what is right."

Introduce object: Let's pretend that we can see God sitting at a desk and writing in his Book of Life.

1. Let's pretend the Book of Life lists the things I have done right.
2. When someone teased me or tried to stop me from doing the right thing, I got an extra good mark.

Conclusion: You will be happy if you do what you know is right.

How many Beatitudes are there? Yes, eight. I have eight keys here. The last key is: "Happy are those who do what is right." They do it even if other people tease or try to stop them.

Let's pretend that we can see God sitting at a desk and writing in his Book of Life for each of us. Here is a page with my name on it [*or select the name of a child*]. Let's pretend the book has a list of the things that I have done right. Let's look back to when I was a child. It says I went to church and Sunday school to learn about God. Here is a time when I shared my toys. Here I helped my mother. I was kind to a neighbor. I tried to be a peacemaker.

Wait a minute, here is something I didn't expect to see. It says I was persecuted for righteousness. I remember when I asked our neighbor to come to Sunday school and he laughed at me and called me stupid. I felt bad when he said that, but I knew I was doing the right thing. Imagine that being added to the list of good things I have done. Here is another one. The girl who lived across the street tried to talk me into helping her take something from her mother's purse. Because I wouldn't do it, she teased me and then she wouldn't talk to me for a long time. I missed playing with her.

I see something else here. In front of the places where I did something right and was teased for doing it there are two check marks. That means they were counted for two good things. The good thing I did was one. Being persecuted, or being called names for it, was the other.

The Beatitude says: "Blessed are those who are persecuted for righteousness' sake, for theirs is the kingdom of heaven." I should be happy when I do the right thing even if other people don't like it, because my reward will be in heaven. Don't let your friends tease you into not doing the right thing—the thing that is kind, truthful, and loving. You will be happy if you do what you know is right.

Attributes of God

How do you describe God to a child? Even adults cannot comprehend him fully. We can, however, give children a sense of God's greatness while also emphasizing that this great God loves and cares for each one of them. Looking at certain qualities of God through the use of familiar objects can help children have more understanding.

9

God Is Love

Object: an electrical outlet and a few small electrical appliances such as a razor, mixer, heating coil, and toaster

Lesson: God is love, loves, and is the source of love.

Outline

Introduce object: Today I want to talk about God and how God is love. I am going to use this electrical outlet to help me.

1. God is love.
2. God loves totally.
3. God is the source of love. Love is what makes the good things of the world work. We can see and feel this love.

Conclusion: I'm so glad God is love.

Today I want to talk about God and how God is love. I am going to use this electrical outlet to help me.

When we say God is love, we mean that he loves all the time and that love comes from him. He has so much love that we say God is love. He has more love than you can ever imagine.

God loves us. He loves us more than anyone can ever love us because he is love. He loves all of us, everything about us, our whole selves. I'm so glad that God loves us so much. He even loves us when we do the wrong thing. God is the source of love, which means love comes from him. Love is what makes the good things of the world work. If I plug this razor into the outlet, what will happen? Yes, it will turn on. It will begin to work [*demonstrate*]. The electricity is coming from this outlet. You can't see it, but the electrical power is there. What will happen if I plug this mixer into the outlet? Yes, it will be able to work also [*demonstrate*].

Did any of you see the electricity? No? Then how do you know that it is there? You know it is there because you saw that it makes the razor and the mixer work. How can we see that the love of God is working? We can see the good things that are happening. We can see people loving and being kind to each other. We can see people helping each other. This love comes from God, and he gives it freely to his world. We can also feel love. The razor buzzes. The mixer jiggles. When I plug in this heating coil it starts to get hot. We can feel the warm, hugging, loving feelings that come from God. Love warms us and makes us happy. I'm so glad God is love.

10
God Is Good

Object: the children themselves
Lesson: God is good; God does good.

Outline

Introduce object: Last time we talked about how God is love.
Today I want to tell you something else about God. God
is good.
1. You know what it means to be good. Show me. God
is good.
2. You know what it means to do good. Tell me. God
does good things.

Conclusion: You can always know and count on the fact that
God is good.

Last time we talked about how God is love. Today I
want to tell you something else about God. God is good.

Do you know what it means to be good? Of course you
do. Your mommy and daddy are always telling you to be
good. Show me what it means to be good. Yes, you are all
sitting very nicely. When you are being good, you aren't
getting into trouble. God is good, but being good is more
than not causing trouble. It is more than sitting still and
being quiet.

God is good because he does good things. Do you know
what it means to do good things? Tell me some good things
you could do. Yes, you can play nicely with your broth-
ers and sisters. You can pick up your toys. You can go to

bed when you are told. You can eat the foods that are good for you. You can be cheerful and kind to people. You can go and get things for people. All of these things are good to do, and they show that you are being good.

What does God do that is good? God gives you the birds and flowers and snowflakes. God makes you so that you can love and be happy. God gives you parents to take care of you. God helps you when you need him. God listens when you pray to him. God takes care of you.

You can always know and count on the fact that God is good.

God Is Faithful

Object: a light switch and an overhead light
Lesson: God will do what he says.

Outline

Introduce object: We talked about how God is love and God is good. Today I am going to use this light switch to tell you about how God is faithful.

   1. The light switch will always turn the light on and off.
   2. God will always do what he says.

Conclusion: Isn't it exciting to read in the Bible about the things God says he will do, and know that he will do them? That's because God is faithful.

We talked about how God is love and God is good. Today I am going to use this light switch to tell you about how God is faithful. What happens when I turn on this light switch? Yes, the light goes on. What happens when I turn off the light switch? The light goes off. On. Off. Will it do this every time I turn the switch on and off? Yes! Will this light switch ever make the ceiling fall in? Will this light switch ever turn you purple? No, it will only turn the light on and off.

Will the light switch always turn the light on and off? Yes, I could stand here all day flipping this switch and the same thing would happen (if the bulb doesn't burn out; but that would not be the fault of the switch). If I returned from a vacation, would the light still go on when I flipped the switch? If I was gone for a year, would the light switch still turn the light on when I returned? Yes, the switch will always turn the light on and off. You can count on it.

You can also count on God to do what he says. God is faithful. When he says he will love you, it means he will always love you. When he says he will take care of you, he will always take care of you. When he says he will forgive you, he will always forgive you. He will do what he says he will do. You can always count on it. You always know it will happen.

Isn't it exciting to read in the Bible about the things God says he will do, and know that he will do them? That's because God is faithful.

12

God Is Caring

Object: a child who can pretend to be upset

Lesson: God cares about you and watches out for you.

Outline

Introduce object: We have been talking about God. He is loving and good and faithful and caring. Sean was upset about something this morning. Come and show us how you felt, Sean.

1. Did you notice that Sean was upset? God notices.
2. Did you care that Sean was upset? God cares.
3. Did you want to do something to help Sean? God does.

Conclusion: God cares. He cares about his earth. He cares about his people. He cares about you.

We have been talking about God. He is loving and good and faithful and caring. Sean was upset about something this morning. Come and show us how you felt, Sean. Were you crying? Did you have a very sad face? Did you sit in your chair and not want to do what the others were doing? Yes, those are all things that show us how upset you were.

Did the rest of you know that Sean was upset? Did you notice that he was crying and had a very sad face? How many of you saw him looking very sad? Maybe you were too busy to notice. God knows when you are upset. He is never too busy to notice.

Did you care that Sean was upset? Did it bother you that he was crying? Did you wonder why he was upset? Did it matter to you that Sean was upset? God cares what is happening to his children. He cares about your problems. He even cares when you don't have problems. He cares about you all the time. He is never too busy to care about you.

Did you want to do something to help Sean? Did you tell him to stop crying, that everything would be okay? Did you try to fix what was bothering him? God wants to help you. You can always know that God cares for you. You can't notice or care or help your friends all of the time, but God can.

God cares. He cares about his earth. He cares about his people. God cares about you.

13

God Is Forgiving

Object: a specially prepared envelope and a picture from a magazine or a drawing showing a child doing something wrong (Prepare the envelope by cutting off the three folded edges of one envelope, discard the smaller piece that has no flap, and insert the flapped piece into a second envelope so that it looks like one envelope, because the one flap is over the other, creating a "secret" pocket. When placing the picture into the envelope, hold the inside flap down. When opening the envelope lift both flaps together to show the paper is missing.)

Lesson: God will always forgive us when we say we are sorry.

Outline

Introduce object: Do you see this picture? Let me tell you what is going on in this picture.

1. Everybody does things that are wrong.
2. We need to bring the wrong things to God and say that we are sorry.
3. He will forgive them and make them disappear.

Conclusion: God has forgiven.

Do you see this picture? Let me tell you what is going on in this picture. This boy is hitting the other boy. He wants to use this ball, but the other boy won't let him. What is going on in this picture that is wrong? Yes, the boy should not be hitting the other boy. God doesn't want us to hit people. And the other boy should share his ball. God does not want us to be selfish.

Is there anybody here who has never done anything wrong? Do you always do what your parents tell you to do and always help others and always share? No, everybody does wrong things sometimes.

What should you do when something like that happens? Yes, when you are wrong, you need to say that you are sorry. When you are wrong, you also need to say you are sorry to God.

When you say you are sorry to friends, they usually say, "That's okay." That means that they will forget what happened and go on playing and being your friends. Sometimes, however, the other person might not forgive what you did. If you broke her favorite toy, she might stay mad at you. Or she might not trust you to play with her toys again.

Sometimes people do not really forgive. But God is really forgiving. He always forgives. It's like this envelope. I'll fold up this picture and put it in the envelope of God's forgiveness. I'll close the envelope. Now it is gone. Do you believe that it is gone? Do you believe that God always forgives? Let's open the envelope and find out. Look, the picture is gone. God has forgiven.

14

God Is Powerful

Object: a strong rope or chain
Lesson: God is all-powerful.

Outline

Introduce object: Look at this piece of rope. Do you think you can break it?

1. The rope is strong. God's power is stronger.
2. You could trust this rope to hold you. You can trust God's power.

Conclusion: I'm happy that the most powerful force in the whole world, God, takes care of me.

Look at this piece of rope. Do you think you can break it? Would some of you like to try? Pull as hard as you can. Do you give up? I don't think anybody or anything could break this rope. I think a truck could even pull a car with this rope.

The rope is very strong, but I know something even stronger. It is the power of God. God's power is the strongest thing you can imagine. God made this earth. He is powerful enough to make the moon go around the earth and the earth go around the sun. He is powerful enough to make the stars shine.

If I made a swing from this rope, would it be strong enough to hold you? How many of you would trust that swing enough to get on it and take a ride? The swing would be very strong. It wouldn't break. You wouldn't fall. You could trust it to hold you. Since God's power is even stronger than this rope, you can certainly trust him to hold you and protect you and keep you safe. Since God's power is the strongest there is or ever can be, you can certainly trust it with your heart and your life.

I'm happy that the most powerful force in the whole world, God, takes care of me.

15

God Knows All

Object: anything that improves vision such as reading glasses, binoculars, a telescope, or a magnifying glass

Lesson: God is all-knowing.

Outline

Introduce object: I use these glasses to help me see very small print.

1. We often need help to see clearly. God does not.
2. There are some things we cannot see at all. God can.
3. There are things we will never know. God knows all.

Conclusion: I'm glad that God knows all about his world and that he will take care of me.

I use these glasses to help me see very small print. They make the print look bigger so I can read it. These binoculars make things that are far away look like they are closer [*if you have a small enough group, each child can examine the effects of the objects*].

There are times when you and I cannot see clearly. We need help seeing things right. I need help in seeing small print. I need help in seeing far away. God does not need help to see. He has perfect vision. He can see everything without help.

There are times when we cannot see at all. I can't see what is on the inside of this book because it is closed. I don't know what is in that box over there because I cannot see into it from here. Can you? I don't know if anybody is in the next room because I can't see through the walls. Can you? God can. Not only can he see clearly but he can see everything. God knows what is going on in his world. He sees more than you or I will ever see.

I can't decide how much noise we should make in here because I don't know who is in the next room to be disturbed. Since I don't know everything and will never know everything, I can't always make the right choices. God does know everything. He can decide what is the best thing to do.

There are many things you and I will never know. We are just not smart enough to know everything. I don't know when I am going to get sick. I don't know when I will have an accident. I don't know how many people there are in the world. I don't know how to keep children from going to bed hungry. I don't know how to fix a broken heart. I'm glad that God knows everything in his world and that he will take care of me.

God Is Forever

Object: a ball of yarn or string, two boxes (Prepare the boxes by placing about half of the yarn or string in one box and pushing the remainder through an x cut in the lid of the box; then force the remainder of the string or yarn through a similar x in the lid of the other box, leaving a couple of feet of string exposed.)

Lesson: God was there before the beginning of time and will be there forever.

Outline

Introduce object: I have two boxes with me today. There is a piece of string coming from one box and going into the other. These boxes will help me tell you something about God.

1. Demonstrate present time with exposed string. God is in the present.
2. Pulling string from one box, show God from before the beginning of time as we know it.
3. Pulling string from the other box, show God continuing into the future farther than we can imagine it.

Conclusion: God was there before the beginning of time and will be there forever.

I have two boxes with me today. There is a piece of string coming from one box and going into the other. These boxes will help me tell you something about God.

Let's pretend that this is when you got out of bed this morning [*pick up string by one box and slide fingers along the string*], and this is the time it is right now while you are sitting here [*pause*], and this is the time you will go to bed tonight [*use up remainder of exposed string*]. God is with us during this time, too.

Yesterday is back here in this box [*pull string from one box*]; so is the day before yesterday and Christmas and your birthday and the time you were born and the time your mother was born and the time your grandmother was born [*continue pulling as you speak*]. Back here is the time before anyone was born and before God made the earth and before there was time. This string is God's life. It goes back way before time as we know it. There is only God. There is still string in the box. We don't know how far back God goes.

Now let's look at this other box. This is where you go to bed tonight [*pull string from box as you talk*]. Here is tomorrow and what you might do. Here is the next day and wherever you might go. Here is next week and your next birthday and next Christmas and when you grow up and when you get old and when it is more years than we can even think of. The string is still coming out of the box. God is still here. I can't pull God all the way out of the box because he will be forever. There is no end of God.

God was there before the beginning of time and will be there forever.

Emotions

Young children can experience very strong emotions. They often, however, do not understand these feelings. It is important to help them know and understand what they experience. We talk about "being in touch with our feelings." This is best begun at an early age.

Jesus frequently showed his emotions. He wept, he was angry, he became impatient. He also loved and brought calm and peace and joy to those around him.

The emotions in this section are presented on a continuum so that the extremes might help identify the feeling as it ranges from, for example, jealousy to contentment. Encourage the children to talk about their emotions as you present the lessons. This will keep their interest as well as illustrate the feeling you are trying to present. Talking about emotions is something everyone, child or adult, needs to do.

17

Fear/Safety

Object: tongue depressors with the word *Jesus* written on them (can also be made from thick paper)—one for each child

Lesson: Fear not, God will protect you.

Outline

Introduce concept: We have many feelings. Today we are going to talk about feeling fear, which means being scared or afraid.

1. Some fear makes us be careful. It is good.
2. Some fears go away when we face them.
3. Other fears are strong, and we need Jesus' help to face them.

Conclusion: The wand will remind you about Jesus and help you to feel safe, not scared.

We have many feelings. Sometimes we feel happy or sad or mad. Sometimes we are afraid. We don't want to feel afraid, to be scared, to have fears. It is like holding an ice cube in your hand for a long time. Your hand gets very cold and it hurts. You want to feel the opposite, to feel warm and safe. Let's talk about fear.

A little fear can be a good thing. We should be afraid of going too far from home by ourselves. This kind of fear makes us be careful. Being careful is a good thing.

Sometimes we are afraid of things that we don't really need to be afraid of. A noise might scare us, but when we find out that is was only a noise, we aren't afraid anymore. We might be afraid of going to the doctor, but we know that the doctor is trying to help us. When we find out that the doctor is a nice person, we aren't afraid anymore. When we face our fears and get to know what is happening, our fears go away.

Some fears seem worse than that. If you think something might happen to you in the dark, you may be afraid of having the lights turned off. You might be very frightened in a storm when the lightning flashes and the thunder crashes close to your house. Some children are afraid to go to new places alone. These fears are strong fears. It helps to talk to someone about them.

I also have something here to help you. I call it a wand. On this wand is one word; it says *Jesus*. This wand reminds you that Jesus is always with you (even though you can't see him) and will protect you from the bad things that frighten you. It can make you feel safe again because you know that Jesus loves you and will be with you. You can hold it and say, "Bad things in the dark, Jesus made you go away." The wand will remind you about Jesus and help you to feel safe, not scared.

I have a wand to give each of you [*distribute wands to children*].

18

Hate/Love

Object: a sliced lemon

Lesson: Replace hatred with understanding.

Outline

Introduce object: If you hate someone, you get a shivering feeling inside, like the feeling sucking on a lemon can give you.

1. Hate, like a lemon, is bitter. It makes you feel bad.
2. When you stop hating, or stop sucking a lemon, at least the bitter taste leaves.
3. Love is like adding sugar to lemonade. Love is a kind, warm, happy feeling.

Conclusion: The more love you have in your life, the happier you will be.

If you hate someone, you get a shivering feeling inside, like the feeling from sucking on a lemon. How many of you have ever sucked on a piece of lemon? Who would like to try it? Is sucking on a lemon something you would like to keep doing? I wouldn't. It makes me shiver all over and pull faces. It is so sour. I don't like it at all. Hating someone is a bad, sour, bitter feeling. When you hate, you make yourself miserable. Like sucking on a lemon, it is something you do to yourself.

You can choose not to hate, just as you can choose not to suck this lemon. You can say to yourself, "This person has a problem and is not being very nice, but I'm not going to let his problem bother me. I'm not going to let him get me to suck a lemon."

Sometimes people say they hate someone when they really don't. It's not a nice thing to say. It makes you feel bad inside when you say it.

When you stop sucking the lemon, your mouth feels funny for a little while, and then the taste goes away. When you choose to stop hating someone, after a while the bitter feeling goes away. No taste at all is better than the sour-lemon taste.

The opposite of hate is love. Love is like adding sugar to lemon juice to make lemonade. How many of you like lemonade? Love is a good feeling. Jesus shows us love and wants us to love each other. Love is warm and kind. The more you love, the more you have to give. The more love you have in your life, the happier you will be.

19

Selfishness/Sharing

Object: a paper airplane (plan ahead to have someone else ask if he may play with it)

Lesson: Selfishness and self-centeredness lead to unhappiness.

Outline

Introduce object: Someone just made this paper airplane for me.
1. We don't like to see people being selfish (demonstrate).
2. It doesn't feel good to be selfish.
3. Jesus wants us to share, to know the joy of giving to others.

Conclusion: Don't be all scrunched up and tight and selfish. Reach out and share and enjoy.

Someone just made this paper airplane for me. Watch me sail it [*have someone else catch it, hold on, and ask if he may play with it*]. No, that's mine. Give it back [*grab it and tear the airplane*]! Now my airplane is ruined. It's torn and useless.

We were just pretending that I wouldn't share my paper airplane. Did you like it when I was selfish and said, "That's mine. Give it back"? No, we don't like to see selfish people.

It doesn't feel good to be selfish, either. When a person is always thinking, "Mine, mine, mine," we say that she is self-centered because she is thinking only about herself.

If you are always having to watch everything you have so that nobody touches it, you cannot enjoy using it. If you never share what you have, others will not share with you. If you keep all of your things to yourself, you will never know the fun of sharing with others. If you never give anything to others, you will never know the joy of making someone else happy.

Jesus knows that we cannot really be happy unless we are willing to share. We need to share our toys with other children. We need to share our time to help others. We need to share our love with someone who needs it. We need to share hugs and smiles. This is what makes us happy. Remember, if you hold tightly onto your toys and say, "Mine, mine, mine," you may wind up with broken toys, but worse, with hurt feelings and broken friendships. Don't be all scrunched up and tight and selfish. Reach out and share and enjoy.

20

Anger/Calm

Object: a candle, a match, and a candle snuffer (You can blow out the candle. Since it will need to be lit several times, it might be easier to light it with another candle or a special candle lighter.)

Lesson: Sometimes anger is appropriate, but it must be controlled.

Outline

Introduce object: Everyone gets angry, or mad, at times. Getting angry is like lighting this candle.

1. Injustice should make us angry enough to do something about it.
2. We need to control anger. It can make us do the wrong thing or use up our candle (life).
3. The opposite feeling is calm.

Conclusion: You don't want to be a hothead.

Everyone gets angry, or mad, at times. Getting angry is like lighting this candle. The flame on this candle is hot. People who get angry a lot are sometimes called hotheads.

It's not always bad to get angry. There are some things that should make us mad. We should get angry when someone picks on a smaller person, or steals someone's food, or kicks an animal. Things like this are supposed to make us angry. When we get angry, it shows that we care that something wrong is happening. Getting angry will make us try to stop the bad behavior.

Most of the time we get angry and then we get over it [*light candle and then snuff it out*]. We get angry about someone being teased, and we tell the person who is teasing to stop. We get angry because something has broken, but we pick up the pieces and get over it.

The problem with getting angry is that sometimes it can make us do the wrong thing. We might get angry with a friend and hit him. We shouldn't hit people [*light candle and snuff it out when appropriate*]. Sometimes we get mad about things that shouldn't make us angry, like throwing a temper tantrum because we don't get what we want. That's a really silly thing to do. Some people get angry too much.

Think of it this way. Every time you get angry, your candle is lit. When you stop being angry, your candle is snuffed out. Pretend your candle is your life and you don't want to use it all up. Save lots of candle for when you get old and might have more important things about which to be angry. Jesus will help you control your anger.

When your candle is not burning, you are calm. Calm is the opposite of angry. Calm people are happier. You don't want to be a hothead.

21

Jealousy/Contentment

Object: a book, a set of markers, new pencils, necklace, or tie (arrange beforehand for a child to help you by holding something that you might like)

Lesson: Be content with what God has given you.

Outline

Introduce object: Susan, I really like those new markers you have. I want them.

1. Jealousy (or covetousness) is wanting what someone else has. It can make us do something we should not do.
2. We can be jealous of people, also. It is a bad feeling.

Conclusion: I am content, or happy, with what I have.

Susan, I really like those new markers you have. I want them. I just have to have them. Where did you get them? Where can I get them? How did you get such nice markers? That's not fair. Why can't I have them? I want them. I don't like you.

When I say these things, what am I being? Yes, I am being selfish because I want the markers for myself, but I am being more than selfish. I am being jealous of Susan because she has them. If I could, I would take them away from Susan. The bad feeling against someone else who has what I would like is called jealousy.

Jealousy is a bad feeling because it makes us be unkind to others and think only of ourselves. It also makes us think about things and having and wanting and keeping them instead of being happy that other people are happy. Jesus wants us to be content or happy with what we have.

Sometimes we are jealous of what other people do. That feels even worse. We get mad when our brother or sister spends time with our mommy or daddy. We feel unhappy when our friend does something with someone else. These sad, unhappy, jealous feelings can get us to act mean to the people we are jealous of. Then we feel even worse.

Yes, jealousy is a bad feeling. I don't want to feel that way. Susan, you keep your markers and enjoy using them. I have some old ones at home that work perfectly fine. I'm going to use them. I am content, or happy, with what I have.

22

Hurt/Forgiveness

Object: a chalkboard of any size, chalk, and an eraser (a pencil with an eraser and paper can also be used)

Lesson: A healthy, happy person is forgiving.

Outline

Introduce object: Most of us like to write on a chalkboard. One reason is that when we make a mistake, we can erase it.

1. When someone hurts you it is as if he has made a mark on your chalkboard. Many hurts will fill up the chalkboard.
2. You need to erase, or forgive, and clear the chalkboard for better things.
3. When you hurt another person and say you are sorry, this helps him forgive you and helps you to feel better as well.

Conclusion: Let's all remember to say we are sorry and to forgive the hurt in our lives so we have room to be happy.

Most of us like to write on a chalkboard. One reason is that when we make a mistake, we can erase it [*demonstrate*].This chalkboard will help me tell you why it is so important to be able to forgive.

How many of you have ever had somebody hurt you on purpose? Did someone hit you or kick you? How did that make you feel? It hurts when you are hit or kicked or bitten. If a friend does this you may get angry, but most of the time it surprises you, and your feelings are hurt, also. How many of you have ever had your feelings hurt? How do you feel when somebody yells at you or calls you a name? It makes you feel sad. You will probably keep feeling bad until the person says he is sorry and you say, "That's okay." Then you feel like friends again.

Now pretend that you are this chalkboard. Every time I make a squiggle on this chalkboard, it is as if someone hurt your feelings. Pretty soon this chalkboard becomes nearly full. What can you do about it? Yes, you can erase the marks. That's what forgiveness is. You tell the person everything is okay, or you just forget about what happened and say to yourself, "It doesn't matter." If you don't erase or forgive, your life will be full of marks and you won't be able to make any nice drawings. You won't be able to enjoy all of the other things you might do with your life. God wants you to enjoy your life. He wants you to be happy. He doesn't want you to keep feeling hurt. He wants you to erase and forgive things that people do to hurt you.

It is easier to forgive if the other person says he is sorry. And it is important to say you are sorry to someone if you hurt him, because to be sorry is to decide not to do it again. Doesn't it make you feel better when you say you are sorry? Let's all remember to say we are sorry and to forgive the hurt in our lives so we have room to be happy.

23

Sadness/Joy

Object: make a paper doll with a sad face on one side and a happy face on the other (a more substantial doll can be made by cutting the wide part off a bleach bottle and flattening it so that a pattern can be traced and cut out)

Lesson: Emotional change is normal. Respond to deep sadness by counting your blessings.

Outline

Introduce object: Do you have a sad face and a happy face? This doll does.

1. Feeling sad isn't bad. Everybody feels sad sometimes.
2. It is normal to move from sad to happy and then back to sad.
3. Being very, very sad or sad too long is not good. For this we need to talk to someone, and sometimes it helps to count our blessings.

Conclusion: To be very, very happy is to have joy. Joy is what Jesus wants for us.

Do you have a sad face and a happy face? This doll does. We all feel sad at times. We are sad when we are sick. We are sad when we lose something important. We are sad when someone gets hurt. We are very sad when a pet dies. We are very sad when something terrible happens. To be very, very sad is to feel grief. When we feel grief, we cry. Crying helps us feel better. We get comfort from other people. They do and say things to make us feel better. Being sad, even feeling grief, isn't bad. It's what everybody feels sometimes. Is there anybody here who never feels sad and cries? There are things like getting hurt or seeing someone else cry that should make us sad.

We feel sad, then we feel happy again. Sometimes we are sad for quite a while, but then we feel happy again [*turn doll as you speak*]. We can be very, very sad or very, very happy, or somewhere in the middle.

Sometimes people are sad and they don't know why. Sometimes people get sad and they stay that way. Sometimes people know they are too sad. If you think you are too sad, or if you are sad for a very long time, you need to talk to someone about it. Jesus says something you can do to help this is to count your blessings. Think of all the good things God has given you and be happy about them.

To be very, very happy is to have joy. Joy is what Jesus wants for you.

Special Days

The following lessons are for special days as they occur in calendar order. It is possible to use some of them at any time, because lessons such as thanking God and preparing our hearts to celebrate our love for him should be taught on a continuing basis.

A New Season

Object: a paper chain (Before you begin, write the name of each child on a separate link. The children could help make the chain.)

Lesson: Each person needs to participate and cooperate.

Outline

Introduce object: I am going to write each person's name on a link of this chain.

1. The links are of equal size. You are of equal importance.
2. Pull, but not hard enough to break the chain. Every person is doing his or her part.
3. Pull harder so that the chain breaks. The paper chain broke, but our group can be strong enough not to break.

Conclusion: How many of you will promise to do your best?

I am going to write each person's name on a link of this chain. Each piece of paper in this chain is the same size, because each one of you is just as important as all the others. It doesn't matter if you are younger or older, if you are bigger or smaller, or if you are a girl or a boy. Each one of you is just as important as everyone else.

Now I am going to pull on this chain. I'm pulling. What is happening to the chain? Each person is holding on tightly. This is a good group. Everybody is doing their share to keep the group together. Everyone is doing their job and helping each other belong. Good going, group!

I am going to pull so hard now that this paper chain must break. We will see whose link is the first to let go. I'm pulling as hard as I can [*two links might tear at the same time*]. There, the chain finally broke. Let's see whose link I broke.

None of you wanted your link to be the one to break. That's the way it should be. Everybody should want to do their best. Only sometimes you get sick or hurt when you can't help it. Everyone should work hard for us to have a good group. Everyone needs to be here. Everyone needs to help the others be happy here. This paper chain broke because I pulled too hard. If everyone here does their best, our group will not break. How many of you will promise to do your best?

25

Thanksgiving

Object: a thank-you card or note (one can be made on regular stationery)

Lesson: Thanksgiving is a time to say thank you to God.

Outline

Introduce object: When someone gives you something, what do you say? Yes, you say thank you. When you can't see the person, you send a thank-you note. This is a thank-you card.

1. On Thanksgiving we say thank you to God.
2. Write children's contributions of why they are thankful.
3. Have children sign their names, or sign for them.

Conclusion: We can pray right now and read the card to God.

When someone gives you something, what do you say? Yes, you say thank you. When the person lives far away, you send a thank-you note. This is a thank-you card. These words say "Thank you." How many of you can write your name? If you can write your name, you can send a thank-you note. If you can't write your name, you can still send a thank-you note by having someone else write your name on the card.

Who knows what special time of year this is? You are right. It is Thanksgiving time. What do we do on Thanksgiving Day? We say thank you to God because he gave us so much. What shall we thank him for? You tell me some things, and I'll write them on this card.

Let me read this back to you. We are thanking God for our mommies and daddies, for our warm houses, for our toys and pets, for our clothes and comfortable beds, for our food and our teachers, and for our church. We are thanking God because we are healthy and because we are loved. Now, who would like to sign this? If you can't write your name, I'll write it for you.

God will be very happy to get this message from us. He will be happy that we know the true meaning of thanksgiving. I want to get this message to him right away. There is a faster way than putting this in the mail. There is a way we won't have to wait for this card to be delivered by the mailman. This better way is to talk to God in prayer. We can pray right now and read the card to God.

26

Advent

Object: a shiny glass ball or mirrored Christmas decoration in which the child can see his or her reflection (you could also get an ornament for each child and write the child's name with glue and sprinkle with glitter or write the name with permanent marker)

Lesson: Advent is the time to prepare for Christmas.

Outline

Introduce object: This is a special decoration. Tell me what you can see when you look at this.

1. Advent is the time we get decorations ready to celebrate the happy time of Jesus' birth.
2. Advent is also the time we get our hearts ready. Our faces reflect this.

Conclusion: We get ready during Advent with decorations around us, with smiles on our faces, and with love and joy in our hearts.

This is a special decoration. Tell me what you can see when you look at this [*children will see themselves or their names on the ornaments*]. I'm going to talk about both you and the ornament.

Do you know what Advent is? It is the time that comes once a year before Christmas. It is the time when we get ready for Christmas. It is the time when we get out all our decorations and prepare for the happy time of Christmas. I love Advent. Everything looks so pretty.

The decoration I showed you will go on the tree. I like it because it shows a very important part of getting ready for Christmas—each one of you. Yes, we need to get our hearts ready for Christmas. Each one of us needs to think seriously about how Christmas is a special time to remember that Jesus came to earth as a little baby. Our hearts are happy because we are getting ready to celebrate Jesus' birthday.

Christmas is not a time for feeling sad or selfish. If you feel that way you will not see a happy face when you look into this decoration. I don't want to see a sad face when I look at the decoration. Let me see your happiest faces. Show me how you feel about Jesus' birthday coming. Christmas is a time to smile and sing Christmas songs and give presents to other people. We get ready during Advent with decorations around us, with smiles on our faces, and with love and joy in our hearts.

27

Christmas

Lights

Object: a string of lights on a tree or held by hand (the kind on which the whole string of bulbs goes out when one bulb is removed)

Lesson: The celebration of Christmas is an event in which we all share and participate.

Outline

Introduce object: The lights on our Christmas tree are so pretty.
1. When we all celebrate together, we all shine.
2. When one person becomes unhappy, we are all affected.
3. Christmas is a time to remember Jesus' birth.

Conclusion: Is there anyone here today who wants to be this bulb?

The lights on our Christmas tree are so pretty. Let's pretend that each light is a little person. The light of the wonderful Christmas season when we celebrate Jesus' birth is shining through each one of these little people. When they all shine or celebrate together, it makes the tree look so nice. It is a happy time for everyone who is shining with the love of Jesus.

Now, let's pretend that one little person here decides that he or she does not want to be part of this celebration. Maybe the person is feeling selfish or angry about something. Whatever the problem, this person is going home to sulk [*remove bulb*].

Wait a minute! What happened to the rest of the lights? Why did they go out? Each of these lights is connected to the others by these wires. When one light goes out, the rest of them go out. Think about it for a minute. When someone around you is grouchy or mean, it takes the fun away from the rest of you. When this person comes back and acts nicely [*replace bulb*], then everyone shines again.

Sometimes people are not thinking about Jesus and how much they love him and want to celebrate his birthday [*remove bulb*]. They may want presents that they should not have and will not get. They may want their whole family to be together, and that might not happen. They may want everybody at their home to get along together, and sometimes people just do not get along.

Christmas is a time to celebrate Jesus' birthday and to think about God. If this is what you expect at Christmas instead of everything you see advertised on television, it will be easier for you to have a happy Christmas and not be grouchy. This person has decided that thinking about the baby Jesus and being part of our celebration is enough to make a person happy [*replace bulb*]. Now we can all shine and celebrate together.

Is there anyone here today who wants to be this bulb?

28

Christmas

Candy Cane

Object: a candy cane (one for each child, if possible)

Lesson: Candy canes can remind us of the shepherds and of finding our way to Jesus.

Outline

Introduce object: I have a Christmas treat for all of you. Did you ever stop to think about why this candy cane is shaped the way it is?

1. Candy canes remind us of the shepherds who were in the fields watching their sheep when Jesus was born.
2. Canes are used for walking. They can remind us of finding our way to Jesus.
3. Candy canes are given to show love and are eaten as part of the Christmas celebration.

Conclusion: Candy canes won't be like just any candy for me again. They give me a lot to remember.

I have a treat for all of you. Did you ever stop to think about why this candy cane is shaped the way it is? Why do we get candy canes only at Christmas? Why are they the Christmas colors? What meaning can candy canes have for us?

We can use our candy canes to remember the shepherds. The shepherds carried big hooked walking sticks so that they could help their sheep if they got into trouble. They could hit and frighten away any animal that would try to hurt the sheep. They could reach out and put the hook around a sheep that had fallen into a hole or gotten trapped in a rough spot and pull it to safety. I want my cane to remind me of the shepherds who heard the news about Jesus' birth while they were in the fields watching their sheep.

A cane can also be used for walking. If a person leans on it, the cane can keep him from falling or help him when he becomes tired. I wonder if the shepherds needed their canes to help them run in the night to Bethlehem to find Jesus. I want this cane to remind me to find my way to Jesus.

We also use candy canes to help celebrate Christmas. Giving them to friends is a way of sharing or showing we love them. Eating them is a special treat we have for Jesus' birthday.

Candy canes won't be like just any candy for me again. They give me a lot to remember.

Object: a new coloring book (or clean paper)

Lesson: The new year is a time for a fresh start.

Outline

Introduce object: Something that I always enjoyed getting as a child was a new coloring book.

1. A new year is clean like a new coloring book.
2. There are no mistakes in a new year, just as there are none in a new coloring book. Neither are there any good works.
3. In making New Year's resolutions we promise to do better in the new year, just as we promise ourselves not to mess up a new coloring book.

Conclusion: There are many things that we can promise to do to make this new year a better one.

Something that I always enjoyed getting as a child was a new coloring book. In this new coloring book there are no marks of any kind. Nothing has been colored. It is clean and fresh. It is ready for me to start to color my first picture. That is what we have with each new year that God gives us. This is a new year. It is clean and fresh. It is ready for me to begin.

There are no mistakes in this coloring book. As you look through it [*turn pages for children to see*] you will not find any scribbles. There are no torn pages. There are no half-finished pictures. There are no ugly marks. The same is true of the new year. I haven't done anything yet that would ruin the new year. I haven't done anything unkind or selfish. I haven't been mean or even cried to get my own way.

I haven't done anything good with this new year, either. There are no pictures colored. I have not tried to do any good work in this coloring book. I need to get out my crayons and begin to color a pretty picture. It's time I got started. There are many good things I want to do in this new year, also. It's time I began doing them.

When I start this first picture, I am going to promise myself that I will make it as good as I can. I am going to color carefully. We make promises like that for the new year, also. We make what we call New Year's resolutions. That means we say what good things we will do in the new year. I am going to promise in this new year that I will try very hard not to get angry or say something unkind. That would be like making a big black mark through a nice picture.

Can you think of something that you can promise for the new year? How about the way you treat your brother or sister? How about helping around the house? How about remembering to pray every day? There are many things that you can promise to do to make this new year a better one.

30

Lent

Object: a room-temperature egg that will be blown out to show the children, a tool such as a heavy needle to poke or gently break two holes in the eggshell, and a saucer to catch raw egg

Lesson: Lent is a time to clean our hearts and minds for Easter.

Outline

Introduce object: Do you know what is inside of this egg?
1. Blow out the insides of the egg.
2. Let love and kind actions push out the unwanted thoughts and feelings from inside of you so you are ready for Easter.
3. Lent is getting ready for Easter.

Conclusion: I want to have a clean heart and mind so that Easter will mean a lot to me. How about you?

Do you know what is inside of this egg? I want to color it for Easter, but I know that I won't be able to keep this egg for long because it will spoil. We need to eat Easter eggs soon after we make them. If there were a way I could take the egg white and yolk out of this shell and use it now, I wouldn't have to worry about it spoiling. Do you know a way? I could crack it open, but then I could not decorate the egg. It would be broken.

I know a trick. I can poke a little hole on both ends of the egg and poke into the yolk inside. When I blow into one end, I make the egg inside come out the other end. Have you seen this trick before? Watch while I do it. Now my egg is empty. I have cleaned out the inside.

Today we are going to talk about Lent. Lent is the time before Easter when we get our hearts ready. Do you remember what we call the time before Christmas? It is called Advent. The two words rhyme. Can you remember them? Advent, Lent.

When we talk about Lent, we often talk about cleaning our hearts and minds so that they will be ready for Easter—just like I cleaned out this egg so that it would be ready.

Can you blow in one ear and have any bad thoughts or feelings come out the other? No. I wish it were that easy, but there are things that we can do. We can say we are sorry to anybody we have treated unkindly. We can push away bad thoughts with good ones. We can chase away a feeling that is bothering us by talking about it. We can do loving things. When I blew air into the egg, the air pushed out the white and the yolk. When you put love in your heart, it pushes out the thoughts and feelings that you don't want.

I want to have a clean heart and mind so that Easter will mean a lot to me. What about you?

31

Palm Sunday

Object: a welcome mat

Lesson: They welcomed Jesus as a king. He had come to be more than a king.

Outline

Introduce object: We have this welcome mat in front of our door.

1. Palm Sunday is when the people welcomed Jesus as king.
2. Jesus had come to be more than king for a short time. He had come to be king in the lives of all of his people forever.
3. This mat welcomes people to our houses, and we invite Jesus into our homes and our lives.

Conclusion: Jesus is here with us, and we all can welcome him.

We have this welcome mat in front of our door. Having a welcome mat is a way that many people have of welcoming people into their homes. Sometimes people have door knockers that say "Welcome," or signs that they hang by the door. Some welcome mats don't have any words on them, but they still mean "Wipe your feet and come on in. You are welcome."

The people in Jesus' day had a way of welcoming, also. They welcomed Jesus into their city. They lined up along the sides of the road and waved palm branches at him. This meant "Welcome to our city." They were also shouting to him and calling him a king, because they thought that he was coming to be their king—to sit on a throne and tell everybody what to do. We remember this day. It is called Palm Sunday. That is what we are celebrating today.

The people were right to welcome Jesus, but they welcomed him for the wrong reason. They didn't understand what he had come to do. He was not coming to sit on a throne. He was coming to die on the cross. He was coming to do something even more important than the people thought. What he did was for all of his people for all time. He was more than just a king for a short time; he was a Savior forever.

It would have been better if the people had welcomed him with a welcome mat like this. It would mean that he had come to them to be king in their hearts. A welcome mat like this invites him into our homes and into our hearts.

If Jesus were coming to our city, would you be on the side of the road to welcome him? If Jesus were walking down your street, would you make sure your welcome mat was ready? If Jesus came to your door, would you open the door and make sure he felt welcome? If Jesus came in your house, would you open your heart to him? Would you welcome him into your life? Jesus is here with us; even though we cannot see him, we all can welcome him.

32

Easter

Object: a cleanly broken eggshell with a paper, ceramic, pom-pom, or wax chick placed inside (glue eggshell back together) or a picture of an egg hatching

Lesson: The Easter egg symbolizes new life in Christ.

Outline

Introduce object: We have eggs at Easter. Do you know why?

1. The egg is a symbol of life. From it the chick hatches.
2. The empty shell is like the empty tomb.
3. The chick is alive. Jesus is alive.

Conclusion: His love will grow in our hearts.

We have eggs at Easter. Do you know why? Eggs stand for new life. Do you know where baby birds come from? Yes, from eggs. How about baby chicks? Yes, from eggs. Many kinds of baby fish hatch from eggs, too.

I wish I could show you a real baby chick hatching from an egg. It is a wonderful thing to see. But we can pretend with this egg. When the baby chick is ready to come out of the egg, it begins to peck at the inside of the egg. The egg cracks the way this one is cracked. Soon the baby chick manages to break the egg open [*open the egg*] and there is a new little chick. If this were a real chick, it would flap around to get dry and make funny little chirping noises to let you know it is alive. Easter is a time for celebrating the new life around us and in us. We celebrate that Jesus is alive, too.

If you look at this eggshell now you will see that it is empty. When a baby chick hatches, it doesn't need the shell anymore. On Easter, we remember that the tomb where Jesus' body was placed was empty. He didn't need it anymore.

We are very happy when the baby chick hatches and is alive. It will grow into a big chicken or rooster. On Easter we celebrate and are happy that Jesus is alive. His love will grow in our hearts.

33

Pentecost

Object: a hair dryer and some objects light enough to be blown away by it

Lesson: The power of the Holy Spirit is an important force in our lives.

Outline

Introduce object: (Explain meaning of Pentecost.) How many of you have ever used a hair dryer?

1. The hair dryer has power to move things around. The Holy Spirit has power to give you kindness, joy, etc.
2. The hair dryer uses invisible air. The Holy Spirit uses invisible power. You can see the results.

Conclusion: You can feel the Holy Spirit's power in your life to give you kindness, joy, patience, and peace.

Have you heard the word *Pentecost?* That is what we are celebrating today. Pentecost is the time when Jesus sent the Holy Spirit to the people of the first church. Jesus had gone into heaven, but he wanted the people who loved him to have power. He sent the Holy Spirit to give them power. You can't see the Holy Spirit, but you can see and feel his power.

How many of you have ever used a hair dryer? It can be very strong. Watch while I turn it on and point it at these silk flowers, paper birds, and small plastic toys. Look at how the power of the hair dryer sends them flying. The

Holy Spirit has power, too. He has the power to give us kindness, joy, patience, and peace. I have never heard of any other person or thing that is so powerful.

What does the hair dryer use to push around our hair or the things that I just sent flying? Yes, it only uses air. Could you see the air? No, but you could see what the air did. The same is true of the Holy Spirit. You can't see him but you can see what his power does. He gives people the power to be kind to someone who has been unkind to them. He gives joy when life makes someone sad. He gives patience to someone who can't be still and wait. He gives peace to someone who is troubled.

If you turn this hair dryer on you, you can feel its power. You can feel the Holy Spirit's power in your life to give you kindness, joy, patience, and peace.

Current Issues

We have a responsibility to talk to children in language that they can understand about some very important issues. Children get their information from various sources. Providing them with the correct information for their situations in a warm and loving atmosphere is a gift we can give them.

The lessons in this section may be better suited for children older than five and more appropriate in a setting other than a morning worship service.

34

Divorce

Object: Cut out four paper figures (cut through four layers of paper at one time so they are all exactly alike) resembling a person (can be a gingerbread boy shape). Sparingly glue or tape two of the figures, one on top of the other, so that they can be pulled apart easily.

Lesson: Children should not blame themselves for their parents' divorce.

Outline

Introduce object: When parents get divorced, it is a sad time. Everyone feels bad. In fact, children feel like Mommy and Daddy are being torn apart.
1. They are my figures; I tore them. It is not your fault.
2. They have been torn apart but not into pieces. They are two separate people who still love you.
3. You can't put them back together again.

Conclusion: Divorce is a hard thing. Just remember, parents do not divorce their children.

When parents get divorced, it is a sad time. Everyone feels bad. In fact, children feel like Mommy and Daddy are being torn apart [*place two figures together and tear through both of them at one time*].

Sometimes the children even feel that they did something wrong. But it is important for you to remember that divorce is not the children's fault. Children do not do anything to make parents split. Did any of you tear these figures? No, you did not. They were my figures, and I tore them. When parents split up, it is not the children's fault. It is something the parents did, not the children.

In fact, these figures have not been torn correctly. I did it wrong. Let me show you how they should have been torn [*separate the remaining two*]. The divorced mother and father have been torn from each other, but they have not been torn into pieces. You need to remember this. If your parents are divorced, you still have two parents. They both still love you. They just don't want to be together. They still need you to love them.

I can't make these two stick again because they are separate. Children often think that they can get their parents back together again. But it doesn't work that way. Once parents are torn apart, you have two separate people. It's best to love and enjoy these two separate parents as much as you can.

Divorce is a hard thing. Just remember, parents do not divorce their children.

35

Death

Object: a picture of a big, beautiful house
Lesson: Death is going to live with God.

Outline

Introduce object: Do you see this picture? What is it?
1. The body dies; we bury it and are sad.
2. The person goes to live with God in his big, beautiful house. It's God's turn to have that person live with him.
3. It is sad for those of us who are left behind, but we have our memories.

Conclusion: People who have died have gone to God's big, wonderful home, heaven, to live.

Do you see this picture? What is it? Yes, it is a big, beautiful house. Would you like to live here? I would. It is such a beautiful place.

Do you know what it means to die? Have any of you ever had a pet that died? The animal gets very still and cold. It isn't alive anymore. We bury it.

When people die, the same thing happens. Their bodies are not alive anymore. They cannot move or talk or even breathe. We say that they are gone, because they will not be alive anymore the way they used to be. We have funerals and bury their bodies because they don't need them anymore. We say good-bye to them. We will miss them.

We also say that a person who has died has gone to heaven to be with God. That person's soul, the inside part that loves God and keeps on living, has gone to a home in heaven to live happily with God. This house has everything anyone could ever want. It is a wonderful place to live.

God's house is an even more wonderful place for the soul to be. It is more beautiful than we can imagine, where it is God's turn to live with the special person who has left us.

Sometimes people die when they are very young. They get to live with God for a long, long time. Others are old, and they will tell you that they want to go to live with God because they are too old or too sick to stay here anymore.

It is sad for those of us who are left behind when our loved ones go to live with God, because we will miss them. God gave us the ability to remember them, and in that way they never seem very far away.

We are sad at a funeral and we cry for ourselves, but we should not feel sorry for the people who have died. They have gone to God's big, wonderful house, heaven, to live.

36

Drugs

Object: a glass about one-third full of vinegar; add baking soda at the beginning of the lesson

Lesson: Taking drugs is harmful. Don't let anyone trick you.

Outline

Introduce object: I'm making something special for you to drink.

1. You wouldn't drink this because it is nasty looking and smelling.
2. Some things that look okay are still bad. Don't put anything in your mouth until a grownup has told you it's okay.

Conclusion: Don't let anyone trick you.

I'm making something special for you to drink. There, it is ready. Who would like to take the first drink? Don't you like the smell of my special drink? Don't you like the color or the way it is fizzing? Why won't you drink it?

You know better than to drink what is in this glass. It looks terrible and it tastes terrible. I can't fool you. You won't drink it.

What is in this glass really won't make you sick, but sometimes people try to get you to take what we call drugs. Drugs can make you sick. Some drugs are medicine for sick people if they take just the right amount that the doctor tells them to take. But some drugs should never go into the body that God gave you, because they will make your body very sick for a long time.

Some people are smart enough not to drink something that looks bad, but they are not smart enough not to take something that is bad even if it looks okay. Does that make sense to you? It doesn't make any sense to me. If something is going to go inside of me, I want to know what it is and what it will do to my body. If somebody gives you something and you don't know what it is, don't put it in your mouth until you check with your mommy or your daddy. Ask first; don't let anyone trick you.

37

Sexual Abuse

Object: a puppet or doll (a puppet can be made easily by drawing or sewing a face on a sock)

Lesson: There are good touches and bad touches.

Outline

Introduce object: My little rag doll has something very important to tell you today. It is about touching.
   1. Good touching makes us feel good. We know it is right.
   2. Bad touching makes us feel uncomfortable. We must tell the person to stop and then tell on them.

Conclusion: God does not want bad touching. God does not want anyone to hurt you.

My little rag doll has something very important to tell you today. It is about touching. There are many good touches. God wants us to love and hug each other. He made us so that we feel good all over when we touch each other lovingly. I like to hold the hand of a little person when we cross the street. I like to set children on my lap and read them a story. I like to put my arm around the shoulder of someone who is sad. I like to hug everybody. This is good touching. My doll's name is Anne. Do you like that kind of touching, Anne? She's nodding her head yes. She likes it, too. Good touching makes us feel good. We know that it is right.

There is also another kind of touching. It makes us feel strange. It makes us uncomfortable. We don't like it, but sometimes bigger or stronger people do it anyway. Anne and I are here to tell you not to let someone touch you in a way that makes you feel uncomfortable. You must tell them to stop. Move away from them. Listen to Anne.

"I don't want you to touch me like that. Stop it. I'll tell my mommy." Anne is right. If someone touches you in a bad way or in a way that makes you feel uncomfortable, tell your mommy or your daddy or your teacher or whatever grownup can help you. God does not want them to do it. God does not want bad touching. God does not want anyone to hurt you.

38

Strangers

Object: a person who is unfamiliar to the children
Lesson: Be careful of strangers.

Outline

Introduce object: Do any of you know this man?
1. A bad stranger will try to trick you and hurt you.
2. A good stranger knows you should not come near him because he is a stranger.
3. God wants us to be friendly, but not to strangers until we are bigger and stronger and smarter.

Conclusion: You cannot tell a good stranger from a bad stranger just by looking at the outside.

Do any of you know this man? No? Then he is a stranger. I'm going to ask him some questions. Stranger, if you offer to give me some candy, should I take it?

"No," the stranger says. "I could be trying to get you close enough to me so that I could grab you. You should never take candy from me, a stranger."

Well, Stranger, would it be all right if I got into your car? What if you told me that my mother wanted you to give me a ride home?

"If I am a bad stranger, you cannot trust me," says the stranger. "I might just be trying to trick you to get you into my car and take you away so that you can never get home again. I might even hurt you. If you were in my car nobody could hear you crying."

Stranger, what if it were very cold or raining hard? Should I go with you?

"No, you should wait for your mommy or daddy. You should never go with me or get close enough for me to grab you. If I stop my car by you, run away."

That's right, Stranger. If you are a good person, you will know that children should be careful of strangers. You won't be upset when they run away from you.

This is where it gets confusing. God wants you to be friendly and kind to people. You would not, however, run out into the street to be friendly with people in cars. Neither should you go up to people who are strangers. They can be dangerous, especially for children. Wait until you are older and bigger and stronger and know more people.

You need to be very careful when you are little. You cannot tell by looking at a stranger, whether the stranger is a big boy or girl or a man or woman, if he or she is a good or bad stranger.

39

Pollution

Object: litter (candy wrappers, crayon wrappers, torn paper, etc.) and polluted water (a glass of water containing oil, coffee grounds, spices, tea leaves, etc.)

Lesson: God gave us this world pure; we need to protect it.

Outline

Introduce object: I found these papers and wrappers on the floor this morning.

1. We all need to pick up litter, even if we did not drop it.
2. We all need not to throw things into the water that will pollute it, and we should ask others to please stop.

Conclusion: God gave us this beautiful world, and it is up to us to keep it clean.

I found these papers and wrappers on the floor this morning. Do you like to see them on the floor? I don't. It makes the room look messy.

Would you pick up these papers if you saw them? Would you pick them up even if you did not drop them? Who do you think picks up these papers if you don't? What if nobody ever picked up the litter? In about a year we wouldn't be able to get into the room anymore. Someone has to pick this up. If the person who dropped this litter didn't know she should pick it up, it's up to us to pick it up. I picked up these, and it is harder for me to reach the ground. Isn't it easier for you short people who are closer to the ground to pick up litter?

I also have a glass of water with me. This water looks yucky because it is polluted. Polluted means that junk in it makes it not good to drink anymore. How does water get polluted, do you think? People dump things in it. You would not drink this water because you can see how terrible it looks, but what if you were a poor little fish and this is the water you had to live in? You would get sick and probably die. Fish are getting sick and many of them are dying all of the time because people dump things that they shouldn't into our water. What can you do about it? You can make sure that you never throw anything into water that would pollute it. If you see anybody else doing it, you can ask them to please stop polluting our water. I think people will listen to a child saying please.

Pollution is a really big problem. Each person in this room needs to help. Each one of you needs to pick up litter and not throw things into the water. God gave us this beautiful world, and it is up to us to keep it clean.

40

AIDS

Object: a first-aid kit

Lesson: God wants us to care for and about people with AIDS, not call them names or cause them more trouble.

Outline

Introduce object: All of us have some kind of first-aid kit at home.
  1. Adults use medicines. Children use hugs and kind words.
  2. AIDS is a bad sickness. We should be kind to people with AIDS.

Conclusion: You can be kind and helpful and caring.

All of us have some kind of first-aid kit at home. Some of us have a medicine cabinet filled with things for treating people who get sick or hurt. I brought some of the things we keep for that: aspirin, bandages, first-aid cream, something for burns, constipation, diarrhea, coughing. I have more things at home in the cupboard. Only adults should use these things, because they have to read the labels very carefully and make sure that the medicines are used in the right way, or a sick person could get even more sick. Except for bandages, children shouldn't touch these things. Children can help with hugs and kind words.

When people get sick, we try to help them. There is a very bad sickness some people get today. It is called AIDS.

Have you heard of it? It is not the same word as in first-aid kit. Most children who have AIDS are born with it. Because doctors don't know how to make people with AIDS better, sometimes other people are afraid of them. It is a good idea to be afraid of the sickness, but we should not be afraid of the people. We should be kind to them, not tease them or run away from them. It's not their fault that they have a sickness.

There are many ways in which you could be kind to a person who has AIDS. Maybe the person is lonely. You could telephone or visit for a short time. You could draw a picture or buy a greeting card to send to the person. Your parents may have more ideas for you.

You won't catch AIDS by being near someone with it like you could catch a cold. You don't need to stay away from the person. You can be kind and helpful and caring.